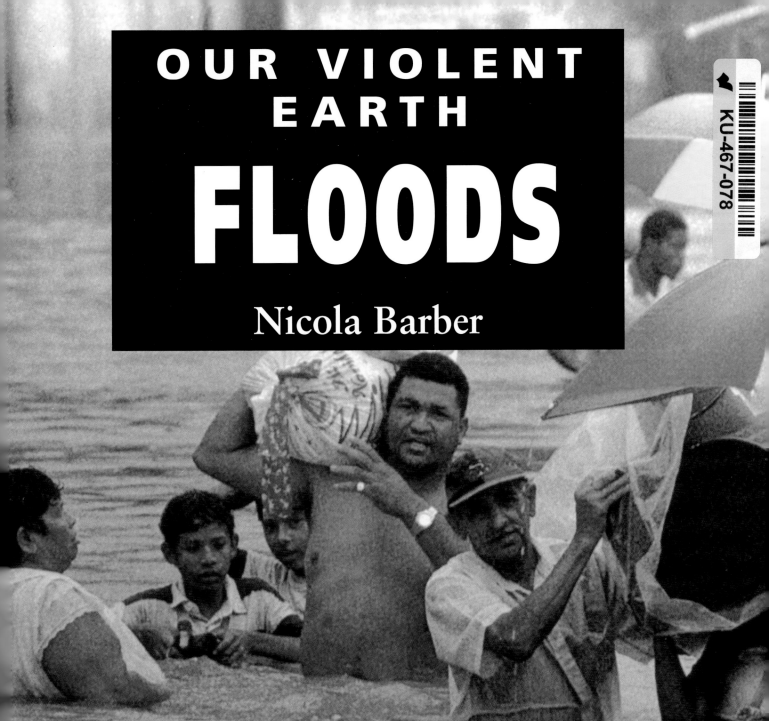

OUR VIOLENT EARTH
FLOODS

Nicola Barber

HODDER
Wayland

OUR VIOLENT EARTH

FLOODS

Other titles in this series:
EARTHQUAKES ● STORMS ● VOLCANOES

Cover photograph: A child waits for help, after floods swept through Mozambique in 1999.

Title page: People wading through the floodwaters that covered Honduras, Central America in 1998.

Contents page: Snowmelt floods in the Netherlands, caused by a warm spring following a cold winter.

This book is a simplified version of the title 'Floods' in Hodder Wayland's 'Restless Planet' series.

Language level consultant: Norah Granger
Editor: Belinda Hollyer   Designer: Jane Hawkins

Text copyright © 2001 Hodder Wayland
Volume copyright © 2001 Hodder Wayland

First published in 2001 by Hodder Wayland,
an imprint of Hodder Children's Books.

British Library Cataloguing in Publication Data
Barber, Nicola
Floods. - (Our violent earth)
1. Floods - Juvenile literature
I.Title
551.4'89
ISBN 0 7502 3510 1

Printed and bound in Italy by
G. Canale & C.S.p.A., Turin

Hodder Children's Books
A division of Hodder Headline Ltd
338 Euston Road, London NW1 3BH

Acknowledgements
The publishers would like to thank the following for allowing their photographs to be reproduced in this book: Eye Ubiquitous 25, 39; GSF Picture Library 38; Oxford Scientific Films 6, 14, 15, 34, 45; Panos/Clive Shirley cover; Edward Parker 22, 30, 31; PHOTRI 10; ßPopperfoto Title page, Contents page 5, 16, 20, 26, 27, 28, 29, 44 (t); Science Photo Library 37, 44 (b); Still Pictures 4 (Jim Wark), 7 (Nigel Dickinson), 9 (Hjalte Tin),13 (Cyril Ruoso), 17 (RUBSAAT-UNEP), 23 (Heine Pedersen), 24 (William Campbell), 32 (Jorgen Schytte), 33 (Hjalted Tin), 34 (Norbert Wu), 41 (Nigel Dickinson), 42 (Gerard & Margi Moss).

Illustrations by Nick Hawken and Tim Mayer

Contents

Introducing Floods

Floods happen when water collects or overflows on land that is normally dry. Floods are most common near rivers or close to the sea.

Flood-plains

The land next to rivers or near the sea is called a flood-plain. The soil on flood-plains is usually fertile and good for growing crops. Flood-plains are often flat.

This is the flood-plain of the Mississippi River, in the USA. You can see that the land is used for farming. You can also see that water has overflowed from the river. ▼

All these things make flood-plains good places for people to live. But people who live on flood-plains are also at risk from the dangers of floods.

Floods worldwide

Almost every week, there is news of a flood somewhere in the world. Floods are the most common of all the natural disasters that affect people. A natural disaster is an event such as an earthquake, a drought or a fire. Sometimes these events happen in places where few people live. Other times natural disasters strike in places where many people live, and hundreds or even thousands of people may die. In July 1997, there was bad flooding in the European countries of the Czech Republic, Poland and Germany. Thousands of people had to leave their homes, and 128 people were killed. In 1998, floods covered three-quarters of the land in Bangladesh.

▲ People use boats to travel through the flooded streets of Dhaka, the capital of Bangladesh.

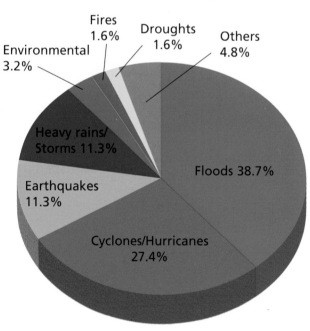

▲ This chart shows how many natural disasters there were in 1996. The biggest slice of the chart is floods.

Floods in Asia

You can see from the chart on page 5 that floods happen more often than any other natural disaster. Countries in Asia suffer more than anywhere else from flooding. In 1991, floods killed 140,000 people in Asia. Many people in Asia live on flood-plains. But in many Asian countries, there is not enough money to build barriers and other flood defences to protect people from floods.

Chinese history

The country that has most floods is China. In China there have been flood disasters for thousands of years. Over 4,000 years ago heavy rain filled the Yellow, Wei and Yangtze rivers. The rivers overflowed, sending water across the massive Northern China plain. The flood-plain turned into a huge inland sea.

▲ Engineers battle against fast-moving flood waters in Germany, in 1991. They are trying to build a barrier to control the flood.

NEWS REPORT

Entire villages are being swept away by floods in China... Hundreds of thousands of peasants are huddling for safety on the top of crumbling river banks.

Adapted from *The Guardian*, 5 August 1998

Flood damage

Floods carry mud, earth, branches and other debris as they flow. Flood waters can even carry large objects such as cars. Fast-moving floods can knock down bridges and buildings. Floods can destroy people's homes, and cut off electricity supplies. They can also ruin crops and pollute clean water supplies with dirty flood waters.

Helpful floods

In some places, small floods happen regularly. For example, in Egypt the River Nile used to flood every year. Many farmers lived on the flood-plain along the Nile. They used the flood waters to feed their crops.

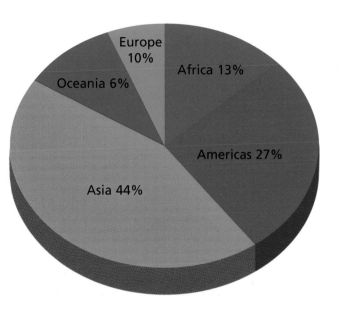

▲ This chart shows the number of floods that happened in each continent between the years 1987 and 1996. On the chart you can see that most floods were in Asia.

This book tells you why floods happen and the damage they cause. It also tells you what can be done to prevent floods in the future.

◄ This picture was taken after a bad flood in Honduras, in Central America. You can see how the flood waters have damaged the buildings.

The Movement of Water

Water is essential to life on Earth. Without water, Earth would be a lifeless planet. Most of the water on the Earth is in the seas and oceans. A smaller amount is in rivers, lakes, glaciers and ice-sheets.

The water cycle

Water is on the move all the time between the air, the land and the sea. This movement is called the water cycle. It begins when water falls from the air to the land as rain or snow. This is called precipitation. More than half of this water quickly returns to the air. Some of it rises as moisture from lakes, rivers and streams. This is called evaporation. Some of it is taken up by trees and other plants, and then given off as moisture. This is called transpiration.

▼ This diagram of the water cycle shows how water moves from one place to another.

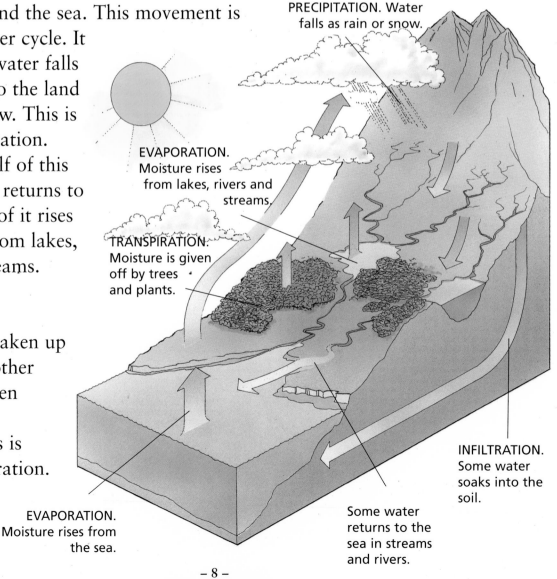

PRECIPITATION. Water falls as rain or snow.

EVAPORATION. Moisture rises from lakes, rivers and streams.

TRANSPIRATION. Moisture is given off by trees and plants.

INFILTRATION. Some water soaks into the soil.

EVAPORATION. Moisture rises from the sea.

Some water returns to the sea in streams and rivers.

▲ After a long drought in Ethiopia, heavy rain starts to fall. The water cannot soak into the hard ground so it runs across the surface of the land, washing soil and roads away.

Infiltration and surface runoff

When it rains or snows, some of the water soaks into the soil. This is called infiltration. The water sinks down through the soil and rock until it reaches a layer that is full of water. This is called the water table. Any water that does not soak into the ground runs across the surface of the land until it reaches a stream or river. This is called surface runoff. It is the main source of flood water.

Drainage basins

Surface runoff water drains into the nearest stream or river. The area of land drained by a river and its tributaries (smaller streams) is called the drainage basin. All drainage basins have different features which affect how often they flood. It can be the size and shape of the drainage basin, and how it slopes. The amount of water in the streams and rivers, and the speed at which the water flows, are also important. Other features are the type of plants that grow in the drainage basin, and the way that the land is used by people. All these affect how the water drains away and how it flows.

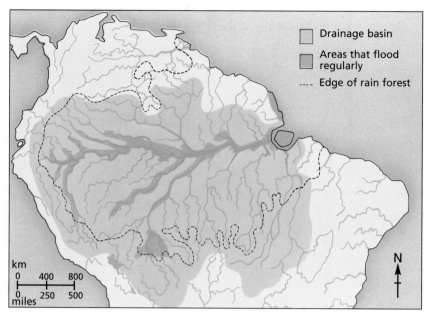

☐ Drainage basin
☐ Areas that flood regularly
---- Edge of rain forest

km
0   400   800
0   250   500
miles

N

▲ This map shows the River Amazon and its tributaries in South America. The drainage basin of the river is shown in pale green. The drainage basin is covered in thick rainforest.

Water flooded this town in Missouri in the USA, when a river overflowed its banks in 1993. ▶

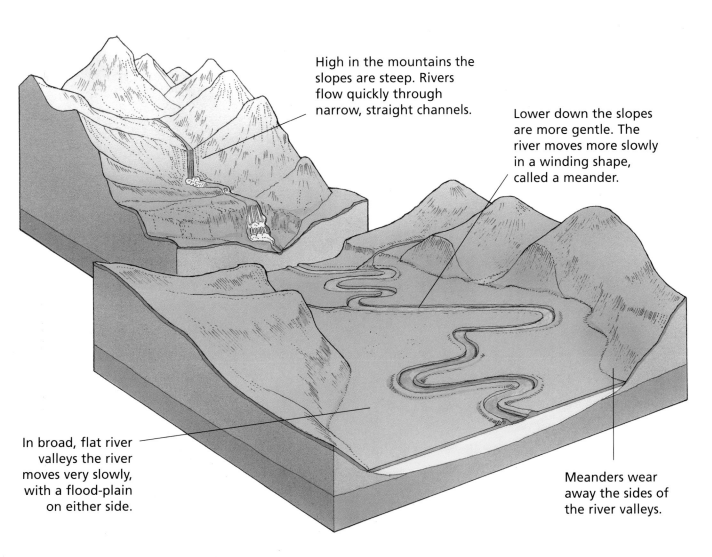

High in the mountains the slopes are steep. Rivers flow quickly through narrow, straight channels.

Lower down the slopes are more gentle. The river moves more slowly in a winding shape, called a meander.

In broad, flat river valleys the river moves very slowly, with a flood-plain on either side.

Meanders wear away the sides of the river valleys.

▲ This diagram shows how a river changes as it flows from high ground to lower ground.

 DID YOU KNOW?

Flooding happens when there is too much water to escape in the usual ways.

Discharge and capacity

The flow of water in a river is called its discharge. Small, shallow rivers have a small discharge. Wide or deep rivers with fast-moving waters have a high discharge. One example of a river with a very high discharge is the Amazon in South America. Only a certain amount of water can flow along a river channel. This is called the capacity of the river channel. If there is too much water for the river channel to hold, the water overflows. This is when floods happen.

What Causes River Floods?

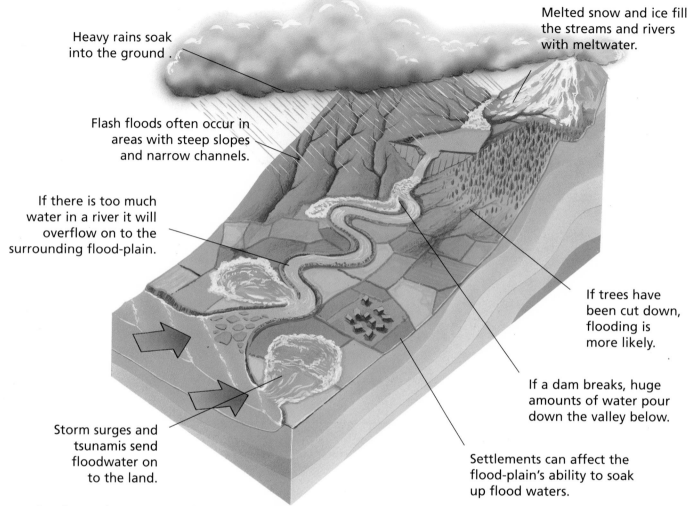

Heavy rains soak into the ground .

Melted snow and ice fill the streams and rivers with meltwater.

Flash floods often occur in areas with steep slopes and narrow channels.

If there is too much water in a river it will overflow on to the surrounding flood-plain.

If trees have been cut down, flooding is more likely.

If a dam breaks, huge amounts of water pour down the valley below.

Storm surges and tsunamis send floodwater on to the land.

Settlements can affect the flood-plain's ability to soak up flood waters.

If a lot of water suddenly flows into a river, there may be more water than the river can hold. This is when the river overflows and floods.

Heavy rainfall

Heavy rain causes most flooding. If it rains for a long time, the soil can become full of water. Instead of soaking into the ground, rainwater runs across the ground into streams and rivers. That makes them too full, and then they overflow. Rainfall floods often build up slowly.

▲ This diagram shows different kinds of flood and what causes them.

DID YOU KNOW?
Heavy rainfall can cause floods lasting for over a week.

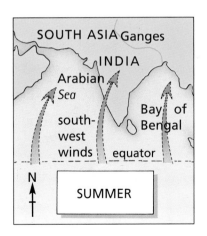

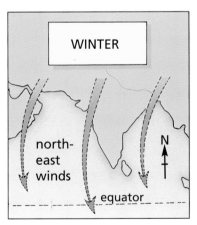

▲ Children sit on the roof of a truck to catch fish in a flooded street in Thailand, south-east Asia. Heavy monsoon rains caused these floods.

SOUTH ASIA Ganges
INDIA
Arabian
Sea
south-
west
winds
Bay of
Bengal
equator
N
SUMMER

WINTER
north-
east
winds
N
equator

▲ In the summer rainy season, winds pick up moisture from the sea. They drop this moisture as rain over the land, causing heavy monsoons. In the winter, the winds blow in the opposite direction. There are no monsoons in the winter.

Monsoons

The word monsoon used to mean season. This is because it was used to describe seasonal winds in southern Asia. For six months during the winter these winds blow from the north-east. For the other six months during the summer, the winds blow from the south-west. These south-west winds carry moisture from the Arabian Sea and the Bay of Bengal. They drop this moisture as heavy rainfall as they move over the land. The word monsoon is now used to describe this heavy rainfall that happens in the summer rainy season every year. The monsoon rains cause flooding across southern Asia.

Flash floods

Flash floods are violent floods that are usually over quite quickly. The name is used to describe floods that happen within six hours of the beginning of rainfall. Flash floods are caused by surface runoff after heavy rainfall. They can also happen when very large amounts of rain fall in a short time, for example in a thunderstorm.

Flash floods are dangerous because they happen very suddenly. There is usually little time to warn people about them. Flash floods are also very fast-moving and powerful. A flash flood can carry huge boulders and other debris in its waters.

A flash flood in Austria in 1988 ripped up tree trunks and smashed this car. ▼

▲ The desert in Queensland, Australia is usually very dry. But a flash flood has filled this shallow river channel.

This map show the area of the Big Thompson flash flood in 1976. ▼

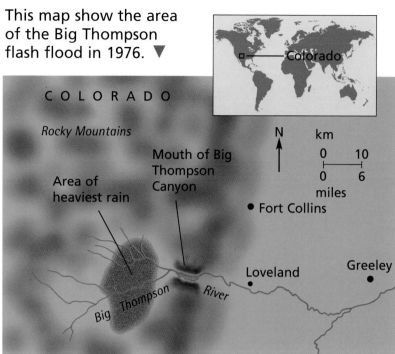

In the USA, there are hundreds of flash floods every year. Some last no longer than 15 minutes. They are especially dangerous in places with steep slopes, where people can get trapped in narrow channels. They are also dangerous in very dry areas. In these areas there can be a lot of surface runoff, and river channels are usually quite shallow.

Big Thompson River, USA

In July 1976, there was a flash flood in the Big Thompson river valley in the Rocky Mountains, in the USA (see the map above). In four-and-a-half hours, over 30 centimetres of rain fell in the river valley. The surface runoff made the Big Thompson River overflow its banks. The flash flood was so powerful that it tore up roads and swept away bridges, houses and people. This flash flood killed 139 people.

Snowmelt

When snow melts it turns into water. The water runs into streams and rivers, filling them until they overflow. This kind of flood is called a snowmelt flood. Snowmelt floods are common in mountains.

In 1948 there were snowmelt floods along the Fraser River in British Columbia, Canada. During the winter there was a lot of snow. Spring came late, but it was very warm and the snow melted suddenly. The flooding lasted for more than a month.

Ice-jams

In some places it is so cold during the winter that rivers freeze over. When warmer weather comes, the ice starts to thaw. But the ice melts faster in some places than others. Sometimes water gets trapped behind a barrier of solid ice. This is called an ice-jam. When the ice melts it releases the water, often causing floods.

▲ This flooded farm is in the town of Tiel, in the Netherlands. The floods happened in 1995 after heavy rain and melting snow filled the Waal River until it overflowed.

Dam failures

A dam is a strong wall that holds back water to make a reservoir. Some dams are huge. If a dam collapses, or leaks, the water in the reservoir pours out. Dam floods are often very violent and can cause a lot of damage.

In 1928, a dam in California, USA, collapsed. It was 60 metres high. The floods from the dam drowned 400 people. In 1963, a different kind of dam disaster happened in Italy. A landslide sent huge amounts of rock and earth pouring into the reservoir of the Vaiont dam. The force of the landslide sent a huge wave of water crashing over the top of the dam. The water rushed down the valley below the dam, killing 3,000 people. Amazingly, the dam itself was not badly damaged.

▲ Workers try to clear up the streets of a town in Germany after bad floods.

 DID YOU KNOW?

In 1889, a flash flood in Pennsylvania, USA, made a dam collapse. A wave of water 23 metres high killed over 2,000 people in less than an hour.

What Causes Coastal Floods?

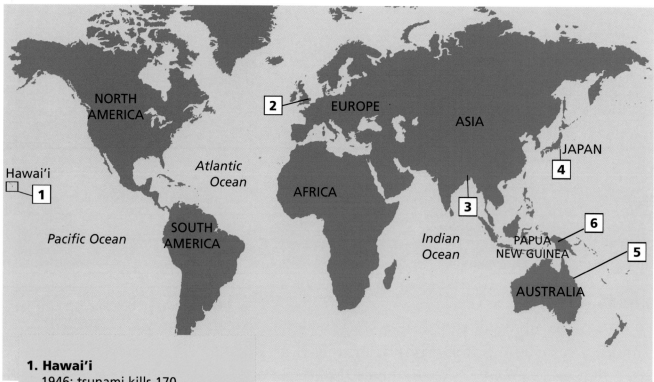

▲ This map shows some of the worst coastal floods and their causes.

1. **Hawai'i**
   1946: tsunami kills 170.
   1960: tsunami kills 61.

2. **Netherlands and south-east England**
   1953: storm surge causes flooding, killing over 2,000.

3. **Bangladesh**
   1970: Cyclone causes coastal floods, killing 3,000.

4. **Japan**
   1896: tsunami kills 26,000.

5. **Australia**
   1974: cyclone causes coastal flooding, affecting 45,000.

6. **Papua New Guinea**
   1998: tsunami kills 3,000.

Coastal flooding happens when seawater pours on to the land. This often happens when there are very high tides. If the land along the coast is low-lying, seawater floods can cause lots of damage. Most coastal floods happen when unusual weather sets off a storm surge. Giant waves called tsunamis can also flood coastal areas.

Most areas of coast are protected from normal high tides by sea-walls. But these defences are not enough if a storm surge or tsunami strikes.

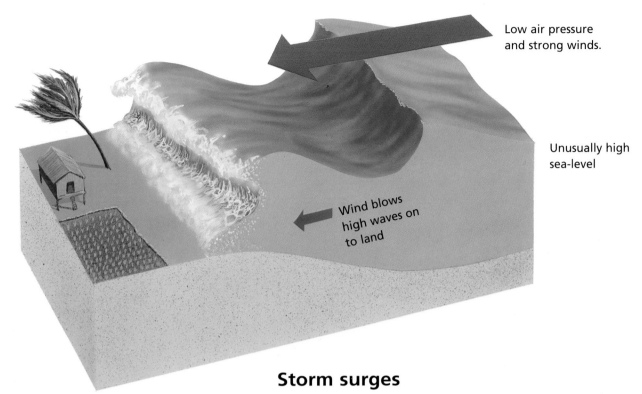

Low air pressure
and strong winds.

Unusually high
sea-level

Wind blows
high waves on
to land

▲ This diagram
shows how a storm
surge pushes the sea
on to the land.

Storm surges

A storm surge can happen when there is low air pressure and strong winds. Low air pressure over the sea means that the air presses down less on to the surface of the sea. The level of the sea can rise higher than normal. If there are strong winds as well, they can blow the sea on to the land. Storm surges can make the sea level rise up to 5 metres higher than normal.

In some places, hurricanes cause storm surges. A hurricane is a severe storm with powerful, spinning winds. It can move at up to 300 kilometres per hour – faster than a high-speed train. In some places hurricanes are called cyclones.

In 1953, there were floods in the Netherlands and England. A storm surge raised the sea level by more than 3 metres. Many people died and over 35,000 people had to leave their flooded homes.

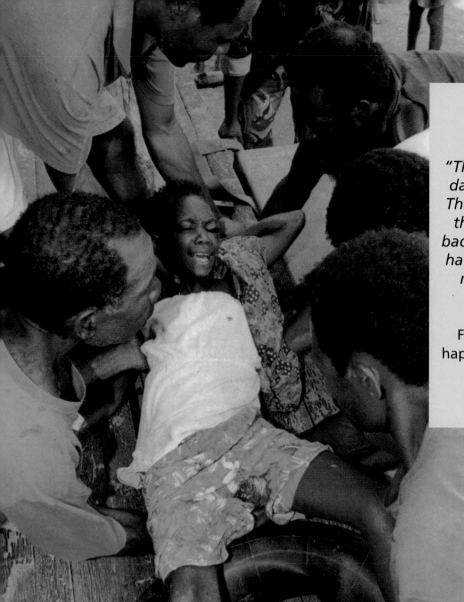

▲ This young girl is a lucky survivor from the tsunamis that hit Papua New Guinea in 1998 (see the opposite page).

 DID YOU KNOW?

In 1883, a volcano erupted on the island of Krakatoa in south-east Asia. The explosion caused waves over 35 metres high.

66 EYEWITNESS 99

"The wave hit in no time at all. It was dark... There was terrible confusion. They were washed one way and then the water turned around and went back again just as fast... Three villages have been absolutely destroyed, with not a house standing. Two others have been badly devastated."

Father Austen Crapp describing what happened when three tsunamis hit Papua New Guinea in 1998

Tsunamis

A tsunami is a giant wave. It can be set off by a landslide. It can also be caused by an earthquake or volcanic eruption underneath the sea. When one of these natural disasters strikes, the seabed jolts. This movement sets off shock waves which travel through the water from the sea floor to the surface. The waves travel across the surface of the sea for thousands of kilometres at speeds of up to 800 kilometres per hour.

Far out at sea, in deep water, a tsunami wave is low and wide. But as it gets near land it becomes higher and higher.

Papua New Guinea

Tsunamis can be up to 30 metres high – taller than 15 basketball players standing on each others' shoulders. When these giant waves reach the coast they crash on to the land.

Papua New Guinea

On 17 July 1998, three tsunamis hit the north coast of Papua New Guinea in the Pacific Ocean. The most powerful wave was over 10 metres high. An earthquake set off the tsunamis. It happened under the sea about 30 kilometres away from the coast. Less than four minutes later the tsunamis reached the land. The huge waves swept more than 2 kilometres inland. They destroyed at least seven villages and killed more than 3,000 people.

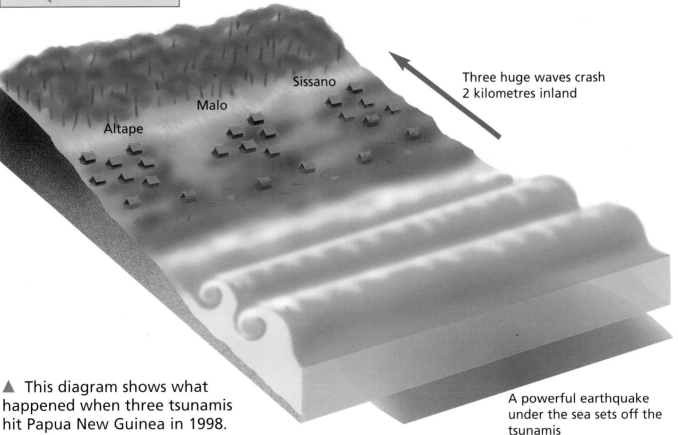

Sissano

Malo

Altape

Three huge waves crash 2 kilometres inland

▲ This diagram shows what happened when three tsunamis hit Papua New Guinea in 1998.

A powerful earthquake under the sea sets off the tsunamis

People and Floods

The Li river, which burst its banks, flows into the Dongting lake near Yueyang, which in normal times absorbs excess water from the Yangtze river. But the lake has silted up in recent years as the population upstream has increased and marshland has been drained.

Adapted from *The Guardian*, 5 August 1998

People have always lived on flood-plains. But modern building and farming methods have increased the chances of flooding.

Subsidence

Around the world, most low-lying coastal areas are slowly sinking. This is called subsidence. But as fast as they sink, these areas are built up again. This happens during a flood. The floodwaters carry mud and earth, called sediment. The floodwaters dump the sediment, building up the sinking land to its normal level again. But if people stop the flooding, this natural balance no longer works. The land will subside and gradually flood with seawater.

◄ The Dongting Lake in China is part of the Yangtze River system. When the river flooded, the water used to overflow into the lake. But today the lake is full of sediment and cannot hold as much water.

 Concrete roads and pavements make it difficult for rainwater to soak away.

Increased runoff

In towns and cities on flood-plains, people have built houses and offices, roads and pavements, so rainwater cannot soak into the ground. There is more surface runoff. Drains carry this quickly to rivers and streams.

DID YOU KNOW?

Every year, floods in India kill more than 700 people.

Deforestation

Cutting down trees is called deforestation. It can often make flooding more likely. This is because the trees in a forest soak up rain as it falls and protect the ground beneath. If people cut down the trees, the rain falls directly on to the ground, and turns into surface runoff. It carries loose soil that is no longer held in place by tree roots. The water and soil flow into rivers and streams, where the soil blocks the water channels.

Flood Disasters

...at 5pm on Tuesday, a mile-long stretch of the 15ft (4.5metre) levee holding back the swollen waters of the river Des Peres collapsed and part of a suburb of pleasant bungalows in the south of St Louis was flooded. In normal times, the river is no more than a narrow stream a couple of feet wide which feeds into the Mississippi.

Adapted from *The Sunday Times*, 25 July 1993

Flood disasters happen where people live in dangerous places.

Mississippi, USA

Millions of people live on the flood-plain of the Mississippi in the USA. When the river floods, it affects a huge number of these people.

1993 flood

In July 1993, there was severe flooding in the Mississippi region. The flooding was the worst for 70 years, and lasted for over a month. It was one of the worst natural disasters ever to hit the USA.

The flood happened because of unusual weather in the previous months. The two biggest rivers in the region, the Mississippi and the Missouri, carried too much water. Both rivers broke through the flood defences, destroying crops and buildings.

◀ When the Mississippi River flooded in July 1993, water filled many buildings.

This is a levee wall, one of the solid defences built to protect people from floods in the Mississippi region. ▼

The damage

The floods covered an area of over 80,000 square kilometres. The water destroyed about 75 towns, and 54,000 people had to leave their homes. The floods killed about 50 people. There was time to warn people about the flood danger, so many people were saved.

What We Learned

For the last 50 years, engineers have tried to protect the Mississippi region from flooding. They have built solid flood defences such as levee walls and dams to try to hold the waters back. But the floods of 1993 showed that these defences were not enough. Some people even thought that the defences had made the floods worse. They said that building a solid barrier in one place only made the flooding worse somewhere else. Engineers are now trying to find different ways to protect people from floods. People also rebuilt many towns in different places, away from the worst of the flood areas.

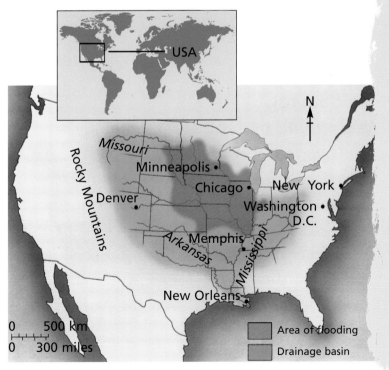

USA

N

Rocky Mountains

Missouri

Minneapolis

Chicago

Denver

New York

Washington D.C.

Arkansas

Memphis

Mississippi

New Orleans

0   500 km
0   300 miles

Area of flooding

Drainage basin

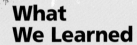

◄ People wade through the floodwaters at this village market in Bangladesh.

Bangladesh, Asia

Bangladesh lies in the delta region of three large rivers called the Ganges, the Brahmaputra and the Meghna. A delta is low-lying, flat area of land where a river divides into many channels and flows into the sea. This means that much of Bangladesh is made up of low-lying flood-plains. Most of the people live on the country's flood-plains. Every year, the summer monsoon brings floods to about a quarter of the country.

1998 flood

People in Bangladesh are used to living with monsoon floods. But in 1998, storm surges made the monsoon floods much worse, and they lasted longer than usual.

The damage

People think that the 1998 Bangladesh floods were the worst in the 20th century. They covered more than three-quarters of the country and lasted over two months. Floodwaters killed more than 1,000 people and affected about 30 million more. After the floods, there were more problems. There was not enough food for people to eat, and diseases broke out.

" EYEWITNESS "

"In October last year there was no monsoon, so the rice harvest failed... Now the summer flood means there will be no harvest at all in November. From now onwards, food kitchens will be the only way to prevent famine, because people in the flooded areas no longer have money to buy food."

Nayeem Wahra, an aid worker in Bangladesh, 1998

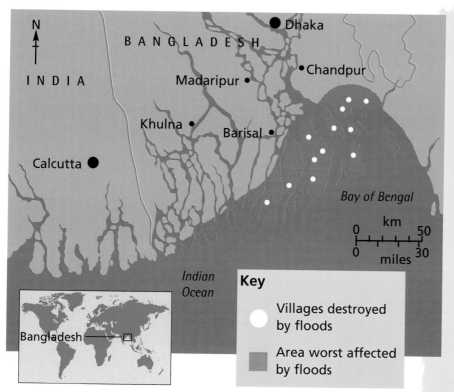

Key

● Villages destroyed by floods

■ Area worst affected by floods

Learning Lessons

In normal years, people in Bangladesh grow enough food to feed themselves and their families. But the terrible floods in 1998 made it impossible to grow crops. Many people went hungry in the famine that happened after the floods. More help is needed for people once the floods have drained away. There also need to be more flood defences to help protect people from bad flooding.

Children collect clean drinking water after the floods. ▼

Hurricane Mitch, Central America

On 28 October 1998 a powerful hurricane struck Central America. It was called Hurricane Mitch. The hurricane brought winds of up to 300 kilometres per hour, and over 60 centimetres of rain. This was more than 15 times the usual rainfall. Two countries, Honduras and Nicaragua, were hit very badly by Hurricane Mitch.

The damage

Hurricane Mitch covered nearly all of Honduras in floods. It destroyed bridges, roads and farmland across the entire country. More than 5,000 people were killed. Over 250,000 people were left without homes.

EYEWITNESS

"We were asleep when the fire brigade came with loudspeakers to tell us the river was rising and we should get out... I grabbed my children and ran. All we have now are the clothes we've been given."

Bianca Rosa Andrade, a flood victim in Honduras, 1998

People in La Lima, Honduras, try to rescue some belongings after floods poured into the town. The flooding happened because of the very heavy rainfall from Hurricane Mitch. ▼

Hurricane Mitch affected about half of Nicaragua. At Casita, the cone of a volcano filled up with water. This caused a huge landslide of mud and water which buried an entire village. The landslide killed over 1,000 people.

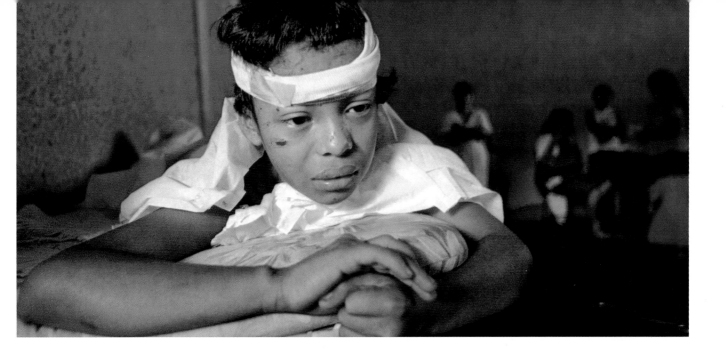

▲ Rescue workers managed to find this child still alive after the landslide from the Casita volcano. The landslide buried a whole village.

Central America

N

Key

Worst flooding

km

0   500

0   300

miles

Caribbean Sea

MEXICO

HONDURAS

GUATEMALA

EL SALVADOR

NICARAGUA

Managua

path of hurricane

COSTA RICA

Casita volcano cone collapsed, causing a mudslide which killed over 1,000 people.

Pacific Ocean

Across the whole of Central America, Hurricane Mitch caused terrible damage. Rivers flooded everywhere, destroying roads, bridges, crops, houses, hospitals and schools. In the region, more than 3 million people lost their homes. It will take many years before these countries recover.

◀ A landslide from the Casita volcano cone killed over 1,000 people.

What We Learned

The region was not prepared for Hurricane Mitch. Weather forecasters said that the hurricane would turn west and miss Central America. By the time they knew that Hurricane Mitch was going to hit Central America, it was too late to warn many people. In the future, forecasts need to be more accurate, and warnings need to be quicker.

▲ A mother and her children stand in the ruins of their house in China. Floods washed away the house during the summer of 1998.

NEWS REPORT

In front of us stand a mother with her baby, her five-year-old-son and his grandmother. Behind them is a scene of utter devastation. Where once there were houses there is a featureless expanse of silt and rubble. They explain what happened: how the rains were incessant. How they were warned to leave their house and move to the flood shelter. How the river level rose 11 m in one day.

And then, they describe the catastrophic 10 seconds during which the dike gave way and the liquid explosion which followed not simply flattening the houses but destroying the buildings and the very ground on which they stood.

Report by Edward Parker for WWF, Central Yangtze region, China, March 1999

China

During the summer of 1998, there was very heavy rainfall across China. The heaviest rain was in a region called Qinzhou. About 173 centimetres of rain fell in June and July. The rainwater filled the Yangtze river and its tributaries. When the rivers overflowed there were huge floods. These were the worst floods in China for 130 years. The floodwaters destroyed an area of over 500,000 square kilometres, and over 3,700 people were killed in the flooding.

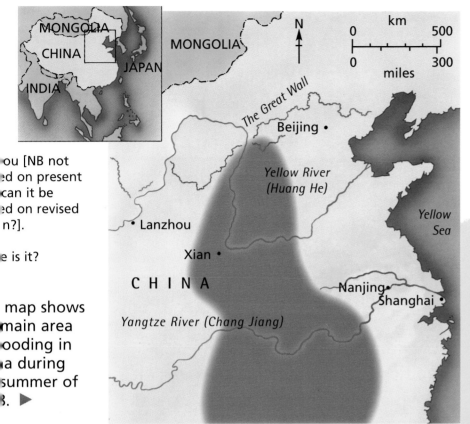

ou [NB not
ed on present
can it be
ed on revised
n?].

e is it?

map shows
main area
ooding in
a during
summer of
B. ▶

What We Learned

There are floods in China every year. But the people who live on the huge flood-plains say that the floods are getting worse. At first, the Chinese government said that this was because of unusual weather. Now they say that there are more flood disasters. They think this is because of deforestation (see page 23). People have cut down thousands of trees in the upper part of the Yangtze River. Now the government has stopped the deforestation. It has also ordered thousands of new trees to be planted.

◀ A man collects bundles of reeds from Lake Dongting. The reeds are used to make paper. But the reeds also make sediment build up in the lake. This is a cause of flooding.

Benefits of Floods

Floods can cause great damage and devastation. But they can also bring benefits, too. In ancient times, many people lived on flood-plains. The Mesopotamians lived along the Tigris and Euphrates rivers, and the Egyptian lived in the Nile delta.

The Nile delta

The Nile is the longest river in the world. It used to flood twice every year because of monsoon rains. For thousands of years, Egyptian farmers have used floodwater from the Nile to water their crops. All over the delta, they have built irrigation ditches and found other ways to move and store the water.

The Aswan dam was built in the 1960s. It controls the flow of the Nile River. Water is stored in the Lake Nasser reservoir. ▼

▲ Water sprays out of a pipe to irrigate a field. This water comes from the Nile River.

The Aswan dam

The Egyptian government built the Aswan dam in the 1960s. This huge barrier now controls the flow of the Nile River. It means that the river no longer floods twice every year. The reservoir behind the dam stores a huge amount of water. This water is used to irrigate the farmland in the Nile delta.

The dam has stopped the flooding, but it has also caused problems. When the river flooded, it dumped sediment on to the farmers' fields. This sediment made the fields very fertile and helped crops to grow. Now all the sediment is trapped behind the dam. Seawater is also creeping into the soil of the delta. The salt in the seawater is poisoning the soil so that crops will not grow.

Mediterranean Sea

N

Cairo

EGYPT

Red Sea

0   300 km
0   150 miles

Aswan

Lake Nasser

• Wadi Halfa

Red Sea

R. Atbara

Khartoum

White Nile

Blue Nile

SUDAN

Lake Tana

• Malakai

ETHIOPIA

R. Sobat

Key

○—○ Dams

|—| Barrages

• Juba

CONGO

KENYA

Lake Albert

◀ This map shows the Nile tributaries, and the position of the Aswan dam.

The Everglades

The Everglades is a vast wetland in Florida, USA. This area was formed after huge floods over 5000 years ago. Many rare plants and animals live in the Everglades, such as alligators, snakes and the Florida panther. The Everglades once spread over 4 million hectares. But in the 1800s, people began to drain the area to make land for building. They made canals, roads, fields and buildings. Today, the wetlands cover only about 2 million hectares.

▲ The Everglades is a huge, shallow river. It is less than 2 metres deep and about 80 kilometres wide.

DID YOU KNOW?

The Everglades is such an important area that it is an International Biosphere Reserve, a World Heritage Site and a Wetland of International Importance.

An important ecosystem

Today the Everglades area is a National Park. This means that the area is protected from more development by people. People now understand that this area is an important ecosystem. This means that they must protect the wetlands and the plants and animals that live there. But millions of people also live in Florida, and they must be looked after, too. People need water, and they also need to be protected from flooding. It is important to think about both the ecosystem, and the people who live nearby.

This alligator is one of the many rare animals that live in the Everglades National Park. ▼

This map shows the position of the Everglades National Park and the nearest big city, Miami. ▼

SOUTH FLORIDA

Gulf of Mexico

Big Cypress National Preserve

Miami

Everglades National Park

Atlantic Ocean

Florida

Predicting Floods

It is impossible to prevent floods. But people can predict when and where floods are likely to happen.

Flood warnings

Scientists use computers to help them predict floods. To do this, they need to know what is happening to the weather, for example how much rain has fallen and how much cloud there is. They use pictures from satellites and from radar to get information about rainfall and cloud cover. A weather satellite flies high above the Earth, looking down on the clouds below. The satellite takes pictures which are sent back to scientists on Earth. Radar uses powerful radio pulses to measure clouds and rainfall. All of this information also goes back to the weather scientists.

HYDROGRAPHS

A hydrograph is a graph that shows the discharge of a river. Flood hydrographs compare rainfall and the discharge of river water. Peak flow is the time when most water is flowing in the river.

Discharge (cubic metres per second)

Peak flow

River level drops

Peak rainfall

Storm flow

Rainfall
50
40
30
20
10

Normal river level

mm   Rainfall Day 1   Day 2   Day 3

TIME

▲ This picture was taken from a satellite. It shows a flooded lake, the Dongting in China, during floods in 1998. The water is blue and the land is coloured red.

 DID YOU KNOW?

By 1985, many towns in the USA had their own flood warning systems.

Scientists also take measurements on the ground. They need to get information about the speed and direction of the wind, the air temperature, and the height of the water in rivers.

When all of this information is collected, the weather scientists feed it into their computers. They make graphs and use other information to forecast what the weather will be like. If they predict that a flood is likely, they issue a flood warning. This warns people to be ready for possible flooding.

NEWS REPORT

"If we had the Three Gorges Dam, the levels in the lower reaches of the Yangtze would not be so high, and the situation would not be so urgent," said Zao Chunming of the State Flood Control and Drought Relief Headquarters, Beijing. Opponents of the dam disagree, saying... that its construction has given a false sense of protection from floods...

Adapted from *The Independent*, 7 August 1998

Protection schemes

In many areas, people have built defences to protect against floods. These flood protection schemes are usually built in places where floods are likely to happen over and over again.

There are two main ways to protect people from floods. The first is to build dams or dikes to control flooding. The second is to make sure people do not live in danger areas on flood-plains.

Dams and dikes

A dam is a huge, solid wall with a reservoir behind it. The reservoir is used to store water. At times of flooding, the reservoir stores the flood water and releases it slowly. Sometimes this means that the flooding lasts longer, but at a lower and safer level.

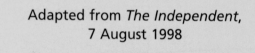

◀ This is the Kariba dam in Zambia. You can see the large reservoir behind the dam wall.

▲ The Thames Barrier protects London from river flooding.

A dike, or levee, is an earth bank built along the side of a river. It stops water from overflowing out of the river. But at times of bad flooding dikes can break, letting the water rush through.

The Thames Barrier

The Thames Barrier was built in the 1980s to protect London from flooding. In 1953 a storm surge hit south-east England and the water broke through protective banks along the river. The Thames Barrier was built to stop this happening again. It has ten steel gates. If floods threaten, these gates can be raised to block the river.

Control on flood-plains

One important way to protect people from flooding is to control where they live on flood-plains. This is called land-use planning. People work out where buildings or roads might make the risk of flooding worse. So building is banned in these places.

Barriers – good or bad?

It is very expensive to build flood barriers such as dams. They also change the flow of the river.

This diagram shows some ways of protecting land and people from flooding. ▼

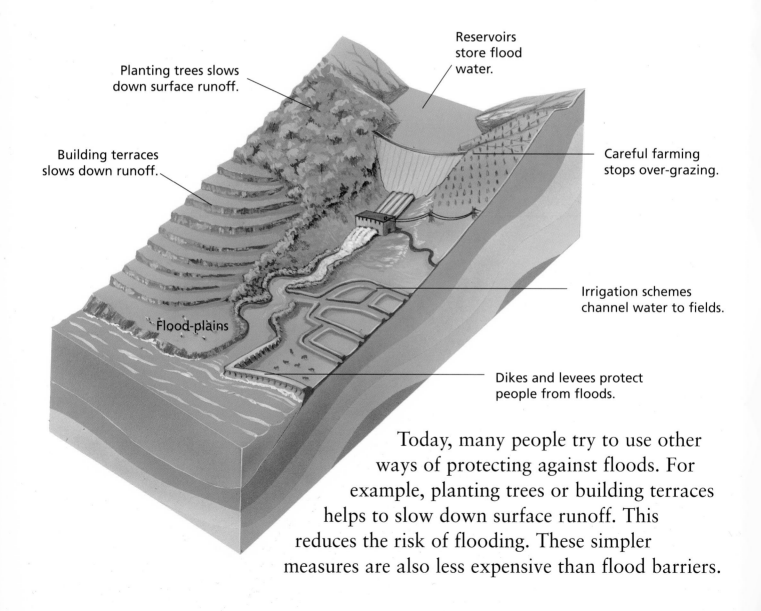

Planting trees slows down surface runoff.

Building terraces slows down runoff.

Flood-plains

Reservoirs store flood water.

Careful farming stops over-grazing.

Irrigation schemes channel water to fields.

Dikes and levees protect people from floods.

Today, many people try to use other ways of protecting against floods. For example, planting trees or building terraces helps to slow down surface runoff. This reduces the risk of flooding. These simpler measures are also less expensive than flood barriers.

66 *EYEWITNESS* 99

"We are expecting cholera, epidemics of dengue fever, diarrhoea, bacterial fevers and malaria... There are hundreds of communities where we have not even made contact... We may never know the... damage done."

The words of a local official in Honduras in Central America, after Hurricane Mitch

After a flood

When a flood does happen, it is important to get help to the area very quickly. After a flood there is often a lot of clearing-up work to be done. The floods often leave behind huge amounts of mud. The water ruins people's homes and belongings. Floodwaters also wash away roads and bridges, destroy farmland, and damage supplies of clean water. If it takes a long time to clear up, people can start to suffer from diseases and lack of food.

During Hurricane Mitch there were heavy rains across Central America. This bridge was washed away by the floods that followed. Damaged roads and bridges stopped rescue teams from reaching people trapped by the floods. ▼

Global Warming and El Niño

▲ The city of Rio de Janeiro in Brazil could suffer from floods in the future.

During the twentieth century, the number of floods across the world increased. Forecasts predict that future floods could affect millions of people in large cities such as Bangkok in Thailand, Hong Kong in China, Tokyo in Japan, and Rio de Janeiro in Brazil.

Global warming and greenhouse effect

One reason for more floods in the future could be the greenhouse effect. The Earth is surrounded by a layer of air, called the atmosphere. The atmosphere contains many different gases, including carbon dioxide. The Earth's atmosphere is rather like the glass in a greenhouse. It allows heat heat from the Sun to reach the Earth, then it traps some of the heat. This is called the greenhouse effect. It keeps the Earth warm. There would be no life without it.

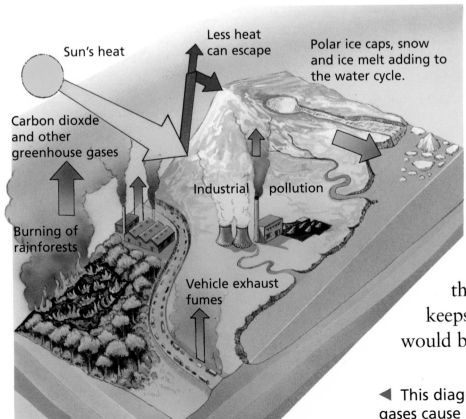

Sun's heat

Less heat can escape

Polar ice caps, snow and ice melt adding to the water cycle.

Carbon dioxde and other greenhouse gases

Industrial pollution

Burning of rainforests

Vehicle exhaust fumes

◄ This diagram shows how greenhouse gases cause global warming.

But scientists know that the Earth is becoming warmer. This is because the amount of some gases in the atmosphere has increased. These gases come from pollution caused by people, such as exhaust fumes from cars. They are called the greenhouse gases. The greenhouse gases trap more heat, causing increased global warming.

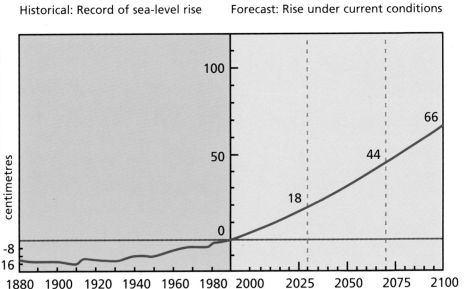

Historical: Record of sea-level rise   Forecast: Rise under current conditions

How much sea-level could rise in centimetres

Year

▲ This graph shows how fast the sea-level could rise by the end of this century.

Many scientists warn that temperatures across the world could rise by about 3 degrees Centigrade by 2100. This extra heat would melt ice from the icecaps at the North and South poles. If extra water from the icecaps pours into the world's oceans, sea levels would rise. This would cause flooding along coastlines around the world. Some scientists disagree. They say that more rainfall would mean more ice, and that the icecaps would grow. They say that sea levels would drop!

Some scientists also think that global warming could make the weather more difficult to predict. There could be more rainfall in northern countries, and in the monsoon seasons in Asia. This could cause worse flooding. But in dry places, there could be even less rainfall. This could cause more droughts.

▲ Children in Brazil walk through dry countryside in search of water. During 1997 and 1998 there were bad droughts in Brazil. Scientists think they were caused by El Niño.

El Niño

The water in the world's seas and oceans flows in patterns called currents. Every three to seven years, in the Pacific Ocean, the currents and winds change direction. This change in direction can last from several months to a year. It is called the El Niño event. When it happens, El Niño affects weather all around the world.

In 1997 and 1998 the El Niño event lasted for a long time. Scientists blames it for weather changes all around the world. In East Africa, Australia and Brazil there was drought. In California in the USA, South America and Sri Lanka there was heavy rain. Scientists think that global warming will make these conditions worse.

The future

We do not know for certain what effect global warming or El Niño will have on the world's weather. But we do know that people can make floods more likely. Cutting down trees, and putting up buildings on flood-plains and coastlines all make flooding worse.

▲ This satellite picture was taken in 1997. It shows an area of warm water near South America (the large red patch). This was unusual. It was caused by El Niño.

NEWS REPORT

This time was a routine flood. It was not… the catastrophic event that strikes St Petersburg once in a century… "I looked at the water and thought, thank God it's changed direction," said Sergei Burdukov. "Because, despite all our preparations, we're not prepared."

Adapted from *The Guardian*, March 1999

Today, nearly half of the population of the world lives within 60 kilometres of the sea. In many places, land is subsiding into the sea. Bangladesh, Egypt, Nigeria and Thailand are all losing land to the sea.

We need to be aware of how humans affect the environment around them. Only then will people be able to deal with floods, whatever the weather.

In 1997 and 1998, parts of Baja, California, USA had twice as much rainfall as normal. The rain filled streams and caused flooding. This was because of El Niño. ▼

Glossary

air pressure A measure of how much the Earth's atmosphere is pressing down on to the Earth.

atmosphere The layers of gases that surround the Earth.

barrier A solid wall.

currents Patterns of movement of water in the seas and oceans worldwide.

cyclone Another name for a hurricane.

deforestation Cutting down trees.

delta A low-lying, flat area of land where a river divides into many channels

drought A long period without rainfall.

ecosystem The relationship between plants, animals and their environment.

El Niño The event that happens every three to seven years in the Pacific Ocean, when the currents and winds change direction.

environment The natural world.

evaporation When water turns into a gas and rises into the air.

fertile Land where crops grow well.

flood defence A barrier put up to protect people or land from floods.

flood-plain The low-lying land next to a river where it floods.

glacier A frozen river of ice that moves very slowly.

global warming The warming caused by the Earth's atmosphere trapping heat from the Sun.

greenhouse effect The effect of greenhouse gases such as carbon dioxide which trap heat from the Sun.

hurricane A severe storm with powerful, spinning winds.

ice-jam When water becomes trapped behind a barrier of solid ice.

irrigation Storing water in ditches and streams and using it to water crops.

levee A bank put up to protect against flooding.

sediment The mud and earth carried in rivers that is dumped on the land during floods.

snowmelt Melted snow that runs into streams and rivers.

storm surge Unusually high seas caused by low pressure and high winds.

subsidence The sinking of land.

tsunami A giant ocean wave caused by an underwater earthquake or volcanic eruption.

water cycle The movement of water between the air, land and sea.

water table The layer of rock full of water below the ground.

wetland An area of land soaked with water, also called a marsh or a swamp.

Further information

BOOKS

A Closer Look at Tidal Waves and Flooding by Michael Flaherty (Franklin Watts, 2000)

The Earth Strikes Back: Water by Pamela Grant and Arthur Haswell (Belitha Press, 2000)

Focus on disasters: Floods by Fred Martin (Heinemann, 1995)

Natural Disasters by David Alexander (UCL Press, 1993)

Natural Disasters: Fire & Flood by Nicky Barber (Ticktock Publishing, 1999)

Natural Disasters: Floods and Tidal Waves by Terry Jennings (Belitha Press, 1999)

Repairing the damage: Fires & Floods by David Lambert (Evans, 1997)

Weird Weather by Paul Simons (Warner Books, 1997)

CD-ROMS

Interfact: Weather (Worldaware, 1999) PC and MAC versions available. Looks at the water cycle, wind, snow, droughts and seasons as well as floods.

Violent Earth (Hodder Wayland Multimedia, 1997) PC and MAC versions available. Looks at earthquakes, hurricanes, tornadoes and duststorms as well as floods.

WEBSITES

For information on weather forecasts and predictions in the United Kingdom:
http://www.meto.gov.uk

For information on flood warnings in the United Kingdom:
http://www.environment-agency.gov.uk

For information on flood warnings and weather in the United States of America:
http://www.state.me.us/mema/weather/flood.htm

Index